George Tybout Purves

St. Paul and Inspiration

Inaugural Address of George Tybout Purves as Professor of New

Testament Literature and Exegesis

George Tybout Purves

St. Paul and Inspiration
Inaugural Address of George Tybout Purves as Professor of New Testament Literature and Exegesis

ISBN/EAN: 9783337172688

Printed in Europe, USA, Canada, Australia, Japan

Cover: Foto ©ninafisch / pixelio.de

More available books at **www.hansebooks.com**

CHARGE.

My Dear Brother:

By appointment of my fellow-Directors it is made my duty
and privilege to welcome you on their behalf to the Chair of
New Testament Literature and Exegesis in Princeton Theological Seminary, and to charge you to faithfulness in the per-
formance of the duties connected with it. We are not unmindful of what you have relinquished in order to accept our call.
We know well the joy and success you have had in the pastor-
ate, and appreciate fully the wrench upon your heart in sur-
rendering it. But, on the other hand, we would not have you
unmindful of what has been given you of God in exchange.
What a choice and fertile field have you here! What a soil
into which to cast the immortal seed of divine truth! What
potential, deep-reaching, wide-spreading influence you must
inevitably exert, as young men go forth everywhere preaching
the Word with the impress of your life and teaching stamped
upon them! Verily, you have been called higher, even to the
position which, at least in my judgment, is the most responsi-
ble in the Christian Church. To be the teacher of teachers,
the preacher to preachers, is henceforth your vocation, your
honor, your tremendous responsibility. Moreover, anent the
persistency with which we have pursued you until we have
captured you, we justify ourselves on the indisputable ground
that in these days of sharp battle, when the very citadel of our
faith is being boldly assailed from unusual quarters, Princeton
has a right to her sons—a right to call them, from any post in
the wide field, for defence and for service. You are largely

your Alma Mater's debtor. Therefore you ought to be, and you doubtless are, ready, in as much as in you lies, to preach the Gospel at Princeton also.

In passing, you will permit me to remind you of the *men* (the word should be written large) whom you succeed— *noblesse oblige.* As you read their names and review their work, you may well be righteously proud. The consciousness that you sit in the chair in which they sat, cannot fail to inspire you to do your very best. It will put you on your mettle.

Moreover, I congratulate you on the *department of study and instruction* which fall to your lot in the chair into which you are to-day inducted. I am not surprised that you "coveted" it and chose it rather than another. "*All* Scripture is given by inspiration of God," and woe to him who sets little store by any portion of it; but the Scripture that proceeded directly out of the mouth of the Incarnate Word and of those who "companied with Him" and heard with their own ears the wonderful Voice, must ever seem the choicest and the dearest, the most potent and constraining and decisive of all— the very heart of the great revelation. It is into this holy heart that it is given you of God reverently to lead the young men who willingly surrender themselves to your guidance. Verily you need to go with unsandalled feet and with prayerful lips. It is told of General Gordon, that during his journey in the Soudan country, each morning for half an hour there lay outside his tent a white handkerchief. The whole camp knew what it meant, and treated the signal with the highest respect. No foot crossed the threshold while the little guard kept watch. The most pressing message waited for delivery until that simple signal was withdrawn. God and Gordon were in communion. You understand me? Let the "*signal*" lie without your class-room door! Let it be understood that you are there not to dissect the Gospel and the Epistle as though they were dead bodies, but to press your way into closest contact and fullest communion with the Living Word! The cry is in the air, "back to Christ." Aye, aye, we take it up and we sound it long and loud—"back to

Christ." Perhaps the cry, as it issues from our lips, is not precisely the same as that of the originators of it—perhaps our
"animus" in it is somewhat different from theirs—but still
we join in it, and we make the welkin ring with it. " Back to
Christ "; and let us make Him the final judge and interpreter
—let us abide by His dicta honestly, fairly, unflinchingly, and
"take His word for it," when He tells us that Moses wrote of
Him, and that Jonah was three days in the whale's belly.
" Back to Christ "—to Him who was and is " the Truth," and
whose testimony must therefore be unerring testimony for all
ages, even to the end of the world; testimony not limited by
his own ignorance, and not accommodated to the ignorance of
the times and of the people in which and among whom He
lived. " Back to Christ "—the Church's one great Teacher, the
world's one infallible Scholar; who stooped indeed, oh! how
low, in taking upon Himself our nature, but never stooped
so low as to misrepresent, or misinterpret, or mislead in order
to accommodate Himself to human infirmity or to human
ignorance.

U nless I misjudge you altogether you need no charge from me
to be fearless of every one in your searching of the Scriptures,
except only of the God of the Scriptures. As one has truly
said, " Fear is a thing which a scholar, by his very function,
puts behind him." You will not be *bound* by the " traditions
of the fathers," but neither will you ignore and despise them
because, forsooth, there pertains to them what is accounted in
some quarters a probable disqualification of their veracity, viz.:
age. " Thou shalt not bear false witness against thy neigh-
bor" may properly be sounded in the ears of those who allege
that this Seminary is timorous in its handling of the Word of
God, because it does not welcome and encourage the hasty
iconoclasm of the day. " Prove all things, hold fast that which
is good." You will not be unmindful or disregardful of the
ancient inscription : " Be bold "; and again, " Be bold "; but
again, and finally, " Be not too bold." Boldness and rashness
are not interchangeable words. It is, it ever has been, the
glory of this Seminary to be bold : it is not, it never has been,

God grant it never may be, its dishonor to be rash. There is a tendency in the scholarship of the day to "think more highly of itself than it ought to think," and consequently to rush, in over-confidence of itself, to much too crude conclusions. What old Isaac said to the boy who was imposing upon him, "How is it that thou hast found it *so quickly*, my son?" may well be asked of certain "re-makers" of the Bible in our time, who are impatient because the Church respectfully declines to accept mere theories for facts, mere guesses for ascertained certainties. Human life is too brief, too brief and too solemn, to be consumed in learning to-day that which is to be unlearned to-morrow. When a prophet comes with a message from God, it must be received and it must be believed, no matter how it upsets even cherished convictions; but when a prophet (self-styled) comes with only his own unproved opinions and conjectures, it is wise, it is right, nay, it is bounden, sacred duty to shut the door against him as "a disturber of the peace."

Again we say, let these Scriptures be searched, sifted, cast into the furnace of criticism seven times heated, and we must, and we will, abide the result; only let not mere "possibilities" or even "probabilities" be reckoned beforehand as the result; and above all, let not the conservatism whose motto is *festina lente*, which insists upon ascertaining whether the bridge will hold before it enters upon the crossing of it, be denominated either bigotry or cowardice or inferior scholarship. You come to your work at a time when there is an increasing and a much-to-be-rebuked disposition in criticism and in morals to "teach for commandments the doctrines of men"; to lay upon the human conscience and the human understanding burdens which the Word of God has not laid; and to demand the acceptance of new-fangled theories with reference to the structure and the contents of the Bible on the ground of the consummate and infallible scholarship to which we have attained. It is the old, old story of bringing these Scriptures to the touchstone of human reason, instead of the human reason to the touchstone of these Scriptures. It is to be withstood with the vigor with which Paul withstood Barnabas. The absolute supremacy and inerrant infallibility of this Book of God as it came from Him, these are to be maintained; or we shall have embarked upon a sad and stormy and fatal sea. Well may we call to mind the prayer which Seneca puts into the mouth of his pilot: "O Neptune, you may sink me, or you may save me; but whether you sink me or whether you save me, I will keep my *rudder* true." Well also may we say of this Book, as the warlike king of his crown: "*God* gave it to me, and the whole world shall not take it away."

But I do not forget that you are to follow me with your inaugural address. It is because I have not forgotten it that I have abstained from any careful or minute description of the work given into your charge—of its character and its scope. This, doubtless, you will yourself outline, and it would be unfair in me to trespass upon the time which is legitimately yours. But this in conclusion: "All Scripture is given by inspiration of God, and is profitable for doctrine, for reproof, for correction, for instruction in righteousness: that the man of God may be perfect, thoroughly furnished unto all good works." This last, my brother: "that the man of God may be perfect, thoroughly furnished unto all good works." The end of all your teaching of the New Testament is to make "men of God," perfect men of God, thoroughly furnished unto all good works, but especially unto that one work to which "the Holy Ghost has separated them." "A learned man," it has been said, "is a torch." So he ought to be, but such is he always? Make the young men who sit at your feet "learned in the Scriptures"; cultivate and insist upon the exegetical spirit in them, which shall impel them to closest, most painstaking, most persistent and persevering investigation and comparison of the holy Gospels and Epistles: but din it at them and din it into them, that they study and dig and search solely for a purpose, viz.: that they may be (1) fuller, better men; and (2), that they may "hold forth the word of life" to others. With the cry, "less learning and more practicality in the pulpit," we have no sympathy whatever. God mercifully retard, nay, prevent the day when reduced scholarship, abridged literary and classical and theological attainment than our Book now demands shall be required for licensure to preach. We have no sympathy with the "short cut into the ministry" tendency. The students here are to be revealers of things to others—they must first learn the things themselves. But still he must be of slow understanding who does not discern the sharp, the imperative demand in these days for preaching straight into the lives which men are living, setting forth doctrine not as an end in itself, but as an incentive and a spur to pure, honest, and Christlike being. The demand is a large one—to preach doctrine into human life, and so save it. But it must be, it can be, it is being met. That you will teach the young men (God grant that the number may run well up into the thousands) who come under your instruction, so to handle Gospel and Epistle that they may be " thoroughly furnished unto all good works," and so be "able ministers of the New Testament," shall be our constant prayer for you, as it is our confident expectation.

Many eloquent, beautiful, and true tributes have been paid by appreciative minds and loving hearts to Caspar Wistar Hodge of blessed memory; but the briefest of them all was the best. It was that which was written in flowers and laid gratefully and reverently upon his new-made grave : " He opened unto us the Scriptures." Aye, he did open them so that the Christ, the living Christ in them, stood revealed. This, my brother, you also are to do—this you will do—" open the Scriptures " so that the young men committed to your charge will see the Christ who is in them, their Alpha and their Omega ; and seeing Him, will say as Saul of Tarsus did after the same sight, "Whose I am and Whom I serve."

God be with you as you take your honored place with your honored colleagues in this honored Seminary of the Church.

ST. PAUL AND INSPIRATION.

INAUGURAL ADDRESS

BY

GEORGE T. PURVES, D.D.

INAUGURAL ADDRESS.

GENTLEMEN OF THE BOARD OF DIRECTORS:

In accepting the chair to which you have elected me in this Seminary, I have been made specially sensible of the greatness of the task which I have undertaken, by reason of several considerations.

(1). In the first place, it requires no little boldness to attempt to follow in the footsteps of the three distinguished expositors of Scripture who have heretofore graced this department by their learning and exegetical skill. Dr. Charles Hodge laid in the chair of Biblical Literature, which he first occupied, the foundations for his later work as a teacher of Scriptural Theology, as his Commentaries on Romans, Corinthians, and Ephesians abundantly show. Dr. J. Addison Alexander acquired during his too brief term of office a reputation for brilliant scholarship which lingers still as one of the brightest traditions of this Seminary. Dr. C. W. Hodge, during thirty-one years, impressed upon the students his own masterly methods of exact and impartial exegesis, his loyalty to the Scripture while thoroughly conversant with every phase of critical doubt and attack, and his profound insight into the historical life of Him who is the Alpha and Omega of the

Word. To his instruction and example I am myself indebted more, perhaps, than to any other teacher, and I learned from him to have so high an ideal of the work which this chair requires as to feel the more timidity in undertaking it. To follow in the steps of these truly great men seems to me so bold an undertaking that only your unanimous call justifies me in attempting it.

(2). In the second place, my experience in the ministry has, year by year, impressed upon me the immense importance for the clergy of training in exegetical methods. That preaching which will not only do the most good, but really be the most interesting to average congregations, is and always will be essentially an exposition of the Bible. But it is exegetical training which secures to the expositor insight into the deeper significance of the Word, richness of thought, freedom from crude and offensive fancies, as well as power of doctrinal demonstration, and these are qualities which can hardly fail to make the preacher an acceptable and attractive spiritual guide of his fellow-men. And, besides this effect upon preaching, it has been my observation that the clerical mind possesses in its exegetical training, so far as that exists, the best corrective of the religious doubts by which it is often itself misled and the means of misleading others. It must be confessed, I think, that many ministers are more occupied with books about the Bible than with patient, scientific examination of the Bible itself. Hence they are led to speculate, rather than to interpret ; to theorize in theology, rather than to grasp in its fulness the contents of revelation. I have frequently noticed that training in precise exegesis of Scripture, strengthening, as this always does, a man's sense of the authority of Scripture, will effectively resist the first assault of doubt, and so prevent speculative scepticism from finding an open field. To aid in training our ministry in the habit of exact and fair exegesis of the New Testament appears to me, therefore, a work of the very highest practical value.

(3). And, thirdly, I turn with the more eagerness to the work of the department of New Testament Literature and Exegesis because of the exceeding interest and supreme importance for the Christian faith of the problems connected with it. Here we deal with the origin of Christianity itself. Here we stand face to face with its historical Founder, and must vividly realize through His life and word, as with every instrument of careful study we examine them, the most real divinity which breathes on us, as on the first disciples, through His most real humanity. Here we are confronted most plainly with the supernatural in history, and are bound to make manifest the impregnable rock of well-accredited fact on which belief in the supernatural, in both philosophy and practical life, must ultimately rest. And here we study directly those shaping forces, whether embodied in men or books, which seem to us most evidently the effluence of God, since out of them all that is heavenly in human life has come. It is true that just now popular attention is fixed with unusual interest on the Old Testament, and I have no wish to exalt one part of Biblical study above another. But the problems of New Testament history and criticism will never cease to command our devotion. As Dr. Sanday, of Oxford, has lately written (*Expositor*, May, 1892): "There have been great ages, 'spacious times,' up and down the world's career—the age of Pericles, the age of Augustus, the years which date from the Hegira of Mahomet or from the fall of Constantinople, the outburst of genius and national life under our own Queen Elizabeth.   But in internal significance, if not in outward splendour, there is no age to compare with that which began in the fifteenth year of Tiberius with a set of obscure events in an obscure corner of Judæa, and which came to its close with the death of the last apostle, St. John." New Testament students have this advantage, that the long battle between those who assert and those who deny the essential trustworthiness of the New Testament as a witness to the origin of Christianity, may be fairly said to have been won.   Of course, sceptics remain and critical assaults continue. But it is no longer possible to bring our Gospels into the second century or for reasonable men to deny that apostolic history was at least substantially what we have always claimed it was ; while every new discovery in Christian archæology, as well as every critical investigation of the witnesses for the New Testament text, drive new nails into the coffins wherein the myth and legend theories of early Christianity have already been laid.   But these results only serve to bring the New Testament student into closer contact with men and forces, movements and literature which evoke problems all the more attractive because the subjects of them are assuredly known to be real ; while a multitude of questions, subordinate to that of the essential trustworthiness of the story, but none the less vital to a right conception of Christianity, are still issues of the hour. The mutual relations and actual formation of the Synoptic Gospels, the historical value of the Fourth, the genuineness of the Pastoral Epistles involving our idea of the apostolic age,—these are specimens of the questions now mooted and of manifest importance. Not that I would by any means have the student of New Testament literature suppose that these critical problems are to command his chief attention. The study of the New Testament itself should be and is to be our main work. But these critical questions must necessarily be discussed, and the relation of them to our conception of Christianity is often so vital that our very faith in the Gospel of Christ and Paul gives to them unspeakable interest in thoughtful minds.

It is, therefore, with these deep impressions of the greatness of the work entrusted to me that I shall enter upon its duties, depending entirely on the promised Spirit of our Lord for wisdom to discharge them, and earnestly desiring to aid my younger brethren in the ministry to present effectively to their fellow-men that Christ and that Gospel which the New Testament reveals.

ST. PAUL AND INSPIRATION.

It is appropriate for me on this occasion to address you on some topic connected with the particular discipline which I am to teach. The department has a double name,—"New Testament Literature and Exegesis." The double name indicates two points of view from which the New Testament is to be studied. The first is historical and literary; the second is hermeneutical. The two, however, naturally go together. They are the two eyes by which the student's mind gains a correct impression of the object. The student of the

literature must be an exegete, and the exegete must be
a student of the literature, if his interpretation of the
Testament is to be complete.   I propose, therefore, to
select an historical centre for my address and use it to
exhibit certain exegetical results which in their turn
will indicate the spirit, in which, as I apprehend, the
study of the New Testament should be pursued.

Now, when looking at the New Testament collection, we find ourselves confronted by one personality in
particular who, next to Christ himself, is impressed
most largely and weightily both upon the New Testament and upon historic Christianity.   I refer, of course,
to the apostle of the Gentiles.   Of him the student of
the New Testament must take particular account.   He
is the author of certainly thirteen, and perhaps of four-
teen, of the twenty-seven books.   His epistles constitute that part of the Testament which gives to it
articulated theological structure.   He was the man
who opened the door by which the world entered into
the fold of Christ.   His mission made the Gospel of
Jesus a universal religion.   And yet he is one whose
right to the place traditionally assigned him has, in various ways in different ages, been hotly contested.   His
own epistles show that in his lifetime itself his apostleship was denied and his mission violently opposed by
many who claimed to be followers of Jesus.   In the
succeeding age we not only find the extreme section of
Jewish Christians continuing to deny his apostleship, but
we find the singular and significant fact that, while the
orthodox church acknowledged and honored him, used
his epistles as Scripture and reaped the benefit of his
mission to the Gentiles, yet it apparently did not grasp
his real teaching, and, if its extant literature may be

trusted as evidence, rejected some of his fundamental
theological principles. Later on, his distinctive theological ideas were for centuries rejected by the larger
part of Christendom, even after they had been success-
fully defended by Augustine and formally acknowledged by the Church; while modern "liberalism" is as
loud as the ancient Judaizers were in its rejection of
Paul's interpretation of the Gospel, and seeks to save
itself from utter irreligion by endeavoring to prove that
this apostle clothed the ethical teaching of Jesus in the
sombre and alien garb of rabbinical theology. Considered, moreover, from the point of view of New
Testament Literature, the personality and career of
Paul are confessedly singular and demand critical study.
He appears on the field, suddenly intruding into the
circle of original apostles, and mastering it by the
success of his work and the force of his credentials.
On any view of the origin of Christianity his influence appears gigantic. Baur called him the creator of
historical Christianity. The very language of the
Church was molded by his vigorous mind, for, as Reuss
(*Hist. of Christ. Theol. in Apost. Age*, vol. ii., p. 9)
says, "It was Paul who imprinted on the Hellenistic
idiom its peculiarly Christian character, and he was thus
in a manner the creator of the theological language of
the church." The student of the New Testament may
feel Paul's influence in the third Gospel and in the
epistles of Peter even as the student of the Christian
origins finds in him a potent factor in the history.
Altogether, he must be particularly investigated. The
question of his authority as an apostle of Jesus Christ
is a crucial one. Its reality, its extent, its inspired
quality,—these are matters which fundamentally affect

our conception alike of early Christian history, and of
present Christian doctrine, and of the Bible itself.   It
may be truly said that our apprehension of Christianity
depends upon our apprehension of Paul.   I have, of
course, no intention of exalting him above the other
apostles or of forgetting their part in the formation
of the New Testament, of the Church, or of Christian doctrine.   But his exceptional history, his peculiar work, his dominating influence, together with the
particular distinctness of his teaching and its intimate
relation to the fundamental ideas which we are to
form of the religion of Christ, make the question of
his authority and inspiration worthy of separate dis-
cussion.

I propose, therefore, to consider the testimony
which Paul himself gave to his consciousness of
apostolic office, his right to the place assigned him in
our Testament, and then to indicate the consequences
which follow from this as concerns our conception of
the New Testament itself.

I. First, then, as students of the New Testament,
seeking simply to know what it actually contains, let us
interrogate Paul himself with reference to his claims of
authority and inspiration.

Rationalistic critics are, of course, under the necessity
of reducing the consciousness of St. Paul to a natural
growth. They cannot admit the supernatural, in any real,
objective sense, to have entered into his experience.   His
teaching and his activity must be explained as in some
way the product of more or less rational processes. He
must, in short, be represented as at once the victim of
hallucination about himself and the herald of world-

changing truth. It is a striking fact that, according to
the rationalistic explanation of sacred history, the
greatest spiritual gains to humanity have always been
the outgrowth of illusion and mistake. For the New
Testament student is confronted, first of all, by Paul's
unequivocal testimony to his infallible authority as a
teacher of faith and duty, and to his special inspiration
by God. This testimony, moreover, is particularly
borne in those great doctrinal epistles, written during
the middle part of his missionary activity, the genuineness of which even inveterate doubters do not deny,—
for the recent denials of their genuineness by a few
eccentric scholars, chiefly of the Dutch school, are based
on too exclusively *a priori* reasoning to be worthy of
serious consideration. It will, therefore, not be necessary for me to discuss the genuineness of his later epistles ; since no essential point of his self-testimony is involved in them.

Permit me rapidly to summarize his statements upon
this subject.

(1). We have from him in the first place repeated and
positive testimony that the objectively supernatural
played a large part and the decisive part in his Christian
experience. He explicitly attributes, not only his personal salvation to the mighty power and wondrous
grace of God, but his cardinal religious ideas to revelations directly made to him. The pivotal fact of his
career was, he tells us, the glorious appearance of Christ
to him when on the way to Damascus, and there can
be no question that he regarded that appearance as objectively real. In connection with that event he claimed
to have received explicit directions for his work and
apostolic authority in it. He was "an apostle not

from men, neither through man, but through Jesus
Christ and God the Father" (Gal. i. 1).   Hence he describes himself as "called to be an apostle" (Rom. i.
1 ; 1 Cor. i. 1), "an apostle by the will of God" (1 Cor.
i. 1 ; 2 Cor. ii. 1 ; Eph. i. 1 ; Col. i. 1 ; 2 Tim. i. 1); an
apostle " by the commandment of God " (1 Tim. i. 1),
" separated unto the Gospel of God " (Rom. i. 1).   But
this pivotal fact was by no means the only supernatural
experience to which he laid claim.   Not to mention
the miraculous gifts which he possessed in common with
other Christians of the apostolic age (1 Cor. xiv. 18),
he asserts that his religious doctrines had been immediately revealed to him.   "The Gospel which was
preached by me is not after man.   For neither did I
receive it from man, nor was I taught it ; but it came
to me through revelation of Jesus Christ" (Gal. i. 11,
12.   So, cf. 1 Cor. xi. 23 ; xv. 33 ; xvi. 25 ; Eph. iii. 3).
Visions, he tells us, were granted unto him (2 Cor. xi.
16 ; xii. 1–4), and future events had in some particulars
been disclosed (1 Thess. iv. 15 ; 2 Thess. ii. 3 ; 1 Cor.
xv. 51).   All this culminates in the general declaration
" that by revelation was made known unto me . . . . the
mystery of Christ : which in other generations was not
made known unto the sons of men as it is now made
known unto his holy apostles and prophets by the
Spirit " (Eph. iii. 3, 5).   Thus a special "grace" had
been bestowed upon him, the grace of apostleship with
all the endowments, spiritual and supernatural, necessary
to fit him for the office (Gal. ii. 9 ; Rom. i. 5, xv. 15 ;
Eph. iii. 3, 7 ; 2 Cor. iii. 5) ; and on the basis of this
immediate divine gift he emphatically declares his inde-
pendence, so far as the ground of his right to be obeyed
was concerned, of any man, even though it were one of

the original apostles (Gal. i. 6, 11). With them he claimed to stand on terms of entire equality (2 Cor. xi. 5; xii. 11), both they and he having been directly invested with authority by the same Lord (1 Cor. ix. 1).

It is manifest that Paul was very far from regarding either the change in his personal attitude to Jesus or his new religious ideas as the result of rational processes of his own mind. Not indeed that his intellectual activity was in abeyance. Far from it. On the truth once revealed he keenly and intensely thought, though, as we shall see, believing himself even in that thought not to be unaided from on high. But his testimony to objective revelations, actually and frequently received, is unequivocal. It is noteworthy also that these consisted not of visions of the other world, of which he has given no description; and very little of hitherto unrevealed future events; but supremely and constantly of those religious truths which men now call theological, but which he called summarily his "Gospel." This, he said, was what had been "entrusted to him" (1 Th. ii. 4; Gal. ii. 7; 1 Cor. iv. 1, ix. 17; 2 Cor. v. 18; Rom. i. 14; Col. i. 25; 1 Tim. i. 11; 2 Tim. i. 11). To use one of his own expressive phrases, "the word of reconciliation had been placed in him" (2 Cor. v. 19). This is not the usual way of mystics or enthusiasts, and it remains for those who deny Paul's self-testimony on this point to explain the psychological enigma which their denial creates.

(2). But, still further, Paul claimed not only objective revelation, but a special subjective illumination of his mind by the divine Spirit, so that he was enabled correctly to teach the word of God. True, he recognizes that all Christians are "taught of God to

love one another" (1 Thess. iv. 9), and we find him,
with beautiful wisdom and courtesy, seeking rather to
urge his readers to a full understanding by themselves
of what was involved in the truth they had received,
than, as he himself puts it, "to lord it over their faith"
(2 Cor. i. 24), for he adds, "by faith ye stand." But he
plainly claims for the apostles, and in particular for himself, as one of them, a special divine illumination, different
both from the objective revelations they had received,
and from the Spirit's teaching granted to all believers,
and on the ground of which the apostle's instruc-
tions were to be received as final because divine. He
does this most explicitly in his epistles to the Corinthians. Speaking of the "hidden mystery,"—by which
he meant the things of our salvation,—he says emphatically, "Unto us God revealed them by his Spirit" (1
Cor. ii. 10). The context shows that by "us" he
meant himself and other apostles; and the subsequent
verses show that this revelation included more than the
objective communication of truth. For he continues,
"who among men knoweth the things of a man, save
the spirit of the man, which is in him? Even so the
things of God none knoweth save the Spirit of God.
But we received not the spirit of the world, but the
Spirit which is of God, *that we might know* the things
that are freely given to us of God,"—*i. e.*, the apostolic
teacher was enabled by the Holy Spirit rightly to apprehend the revelation given to him. Hence he could say
without audacity, "we have the mind of Christ" (1 Cor.
ii. 16). Hence also in the second epistle, speaking of
his apostolic authority and defending himself against
detractors, he could write, "we preach Christ Jesus as
Lord, and ourselves as your servants for Jesus' sake,—see-

ing it is God that said, Light shall shine out of darkness, who shined in our hearts to give the light of the knowledge of the glory of God in the face of Jesus Christ" (2 Cor. iv. 6). Though these words may be properly applied to all believers, the reader cannot fail to see that Paul applied them in a special sense to himself as a divinely enlightened teacher, as one in whose mind the Almighty Creator of all light had shined for the express purpose of making the knowledge of His glory in the face of Christ known to other men; and this was to such an extent true that he could also write, " if any man thinketh himself to be a prophet or spiritual, let him take knowledge of the things that I write unto you, that they are the commandments of the Lord" (1 Cor. xiv. 35).

Moreover we find him, in 1 Cor. vii., where he deals with the subject of marriage, carefully distinguishing between the known command of Christ about divorce ; his own command on the subject, which he makes as obligatory as the Lord's ; and his advice to certain of them in view of "the present distress." Even his advice was inspired, for, after giving it, he adds with a touch of irony, "I think that I also have the Spirit of God." Nevertheless it was advice, not command ; and the ability to thus discriminate between what was obligatory and what was advisable indicates a perfectly clear perception of what, apart from specific revelations, he was authorized by God to require of them and what not.

So far then as his own testimony goes, Paul asserted not only a divine commission and divine revelations, but such an illumination by the Holy Spirit that he could say, " God doth beseech you by us" (2 Cor. v. 20), and "Christ speaketh in me" (2 Cor. xiii. 3).

(3). It is little to observe after this that the apostle
claimed authority over the faith and conduct of Christians. Though he associates other brethren with him
in his epistles, he always puts himself above them (1
Thess. i. 1 ; 2 Thess. i. 1 ; 2 Cor. i. 1 ; Col. i. 1).
Though both Apollos and he were ministers of Christ,
he and not Apollos was a founder of the Church: and
his language conveys the idea that not merely because
he was in Corinth before Apollos, but because he held
a different office, was he the founder of that Church (1
Cor. iii. 10–14). He habitually speaks of his "Gospel"
in terms applicable to nothing less than the full manifestation of divine, saving truth (1 Thess. i. 5 ; 2 Thess.
ii. 14 ; 2 Cor. iv. 3, 4 ; Rom. ii. 16, xv. 25 ; 2 Tim. ii. 8).
In fact he identifies it with "the word of the Lord" (1
Thess. i. 8, ii. 13 ; 2 Thess. iii. 1), declaring in one place
(1 Thess. ii. 13), "we thank God that when ye received
from us the word of the message, even the word of God,
ye accepted it, not as the word of men, but as it is in
truth the word of God, which also worketh in you that
believe." He warns against any who taught contrary to
what they had received from him, yea though the teacher
were an angel from heaven or the apostle himself (2
Thess. ii. 2 ; Gal. i. 8, 9). Alike in matters of faith and
conduct does he speak in an unfaltering tone of absolute command.

(4). It is more important to observe that he attached
the same authority to his letters as to his oral teaching,
and to the verbal form in which his teaching was expressed no less than to the truth itself. Besides direct-
ing the reading and circulation of his epistles (1 Thess.
iv. 27 ; Col. iv. 16, 17), he says expressly (2 Thess. ii. 15),
"brethren, stand fast and hold the traditions which ye

were taught whether by word or by epistle of ours." As
to the verbal form of his teaching, his language is like-
wise unmistakable (1 Cor. ii. 13). " Which things also,"
—*i. e.*, the knowledge given to the apostles by the
Spirit,—" we speak not in words which man's wisdom
teacheth, but which the Spirit teacheth,—combining
spiritual things with spiritual." That this statement is
to be interpreted in any such way as to make the apostle represent himself as a mechanical, unthinking agent
of the Spirit is both disproved by all the phenomena of
his writings, and is positively forbidden by the phrase itself, " words which the Spirit *teacheth* "; for a machine
cannot be taught, it can be only used. But it is equally
plain that Paul felt even the verbal forms, in which with
the full use of his own intellect and heart, and often in
most characteristic and peculiar style, he uttered the
message that God had given him, to have been also
determined for him by the Spirit. He represented his
whole communication to men as " pneumatic,"—as the
Spirit's work throughout ; and therefore in all its elements the communication to men not of Paul's thought,
—that was only the medium,—but the communication
of the mind and will of God. As certainly as the
phrase, " words which man's wisdom teacheth," describes
the rhetorical dress and mode of argument and literary
style which Hellenic culture would have suggested, so
certainly does he mean in the corresponding phrase,
" words which the Spirit teacheth," to say that the
rhetoric and the argument and the style which he did
employ were in some way, which he does not explain,
suggested, indicated, brought to his mind by the Holy
Spirit.

(5). At the same time, be it noted, there never was a

more living writer than Paul, and his testimony is
equally clear that, with all the authority and divine
guidance which he claimed, he was always himself.
His self-consciousness, in fact, is very marked, since he
regarded himself as a typical example of grace, and
since he was compelled to defend his character and his
claims. His personality was intense. The " I, Paul, say
unto you" is very frequent. He testifies to nothing
mechanical in the operations of divine power within his
mind, but quite to the contrary. His writings themselves bear sufficient witness to his intellectual activity,
his strong and sensitive emotions, his quickness to discern the practical relations of his teaching. His testimony to the living reality of his experience under
grace, and while the subject of revealing and inspiring
power, is as clear as is his testimony to that power itself.
And to this should be added the remark that he recognized the limitations of his knowledge. The Spirit did
not always quicken his memory, for he writes of his life
in Corinth : " I baptized also the household of Stepha-
nas : besides I know not whether I baptized any other"
(1 Cor. i. 16). Neither did he claim perfect compre-
hension of the truth, for he could say, "Now I know
in part; but then shall I know even as also I am
known" (1 Cor. xiii. 11). But this confession of limits
to knowledge only makes the more significant his asser-
tions of clear and authoritative knowledge as to what
had been given him to affirm and teach. It indicates a
calm and sober appreciation of just what God authorized
him to say and what he did not, which is at the farthest
possible remove from either a machine or an enthusiast.
" This treasure," he says, speaking of the divine light
which God had made to shine within his mind, " we

have in earthen vessels, that the exceeding greatness of the
power may be of God and not of us" (2 Cor. iv. 7).   By
the "earthen vessel" he did not mean, as he has sometimes been interpreted, the human element in his writings,
their words and arguments.   These, as we have seen, he
regarded as part of the treasure itself.   But, as the context shows, he meant by "the earthen vessel," the
external trials and the personal misfortunes of his life,—
for he was "always," he added, "bearing about in his
body the dying of the Lord Jesus, that the life also of
Jesus might be made manifest in our mortal flesh."   To
the Jews a renegade, to the Athenians a babbler,
"the offscouring of the earth" in the eyes of the busy,
fighting, cultured, careless Roman world,—Paul claimed
that he possessed a gift from Almighty God which
made him a true prophet of Israel, an unerring
teacher of the wise, and an authoritative expounder of
the only way of salvation for mankind.

Such I believe to be a fair statement of Paul's
apostolic consciousness as exegesis gives it to us.   Thus
he appears on the field of New Testament literature.
This is the only Paul of which we know.   It may be
conceivable that he was an utterly mistaken man, but
he cannot be treated as pretending to be different from
what we have described.

II.   Can, then, these claims be justified to us so that,
as students of New Testament literature, we may accept
Paul's epistles as a constituent part of the sacred Scriptures, and Paul himself as the authorized exponent of
genuine Christianity which he claimed to be ?

We do not hesitate to say that the objections brought
by avowed naturalism are to be immediately set aside.

We come to the examination of New Testament literature, believing in the possibility of miracles, and even,
under certain circumstances, in their probability. Above
all, we come as convinced believers in an historical
incarnation and resurrection. Our belief in this may
be defended quite independently of Paul's claims to
authority and inspiration. He may be regarded as mistaken in these and yet may constitute one of the many
witnesses to the original belief of the primitive church,
and, as such, one of many facts which only an actual
incarnation and resurrection can explain. Fairness
does not require us, therefore, to profess want of conviction upon these points. For belief in the incarnation and resurrection does not necessarily carry with it
the admission of Paul's specific claims, while unbelief
does carry with it the denial of them.

In the hands of naturalism, moreover, not only must
Paul appear a singularly deluded man and his conver-
sion remain an unexplained enigma, but he can scarcely
be made to justify the place he has occupied among
the leaders of mankind. When Professor Pfleiderer
concludes that "the specially Christian and permanent
element of Paulinism" was the fact "that it was an
influence bringing freedom and inward depth to the
religious life, delivering men from all externalities and
uniting them directly with God" (*Hibbert Lectures*,
1885, p. 287); when Mr. Arnold, trying to show why
Protestantism should still uphold the honor of its
favorite apostle, makes Paul's essential merit to have
been that he was possessed with a zeal for righteousness (*St. Paul and Protestantism, passim*), we in-
stinctively ask why, of all the advocates of religious
liberty and righteousness, this man should occupy a

unique position in history. Manifestly such praise is but the cloak which conceals the hand of the assassin. Not by these qualities alone has Paul actually exerted his decisive influence on mankind.

The New Testament student, therefore, is not to approach the subject without faith in an historical revelation of God through Jesus Christ. He is rather to inquire whether, assuming the fact of a supernatural revelation, the extraordinary and specific claims of this intruder into the original circle of disciples ought to be acknowledged.

Without attempting to do more than give an outline of the argument, the following reasons appear to us conclusive.

The particular credentials by which Paul himself appealed to his own converts are either beyond our power of testing or are not sufficiently explicit for our present purpose. They consisted in the miraculous powers with which he was endowed, and, above all, in the Holy Spirit accompanying his ministry and sealing his word to the hearts of God's elect (1 Cor. xii. 12; 1 Thess. i. 5; 1 Cor. ii. 4–5). The former we cannot directly verify. The witness of the Spirit to his teaching we must certainly, if Christian men, feel. It has been largely because the experience of Christian life bears so much testimony to the essential truth of his doctrine that the church, even when willing, has not been able, to deny it. Nevertheless, the Spirit's testimony is only explicit with reference to Paul's fundamental doctrines. On the basis of that we might indeed infer the validity of all his claims. But as a matter of fact, the form in which he couched his teaching has been impugned even by those who profess to acknowledge the latter, and the dimness of the Christian consciousness is such that it is easy even for Christian men to question the full validity and reality of all that Paul asserts about himself. But the student of New Testament literature may, we think, conclusively furnish two other lines of proof ; first, the fact of Paul's recognition as an apostle by the original church ; and secondly, the internal relation which his teaching bears to the rest of Scripture.

(1). His recognition by the original Church is a fact of first value because it affords conclusive evidence that his claims were admitted by the other apostles and thus that the first founders of the Church confessed the validity of his credentials.

On this point, as you are aware, the modern critical assault has been directed ; and rightly so, if the supernatural character of Christianity is to be disproved. Baur thrust his knife into the vital part of the system when he undertook to prove the original antagonism of Paul and "the twelve," and to explain Catholic Christianity as the reconciliation, 150 years later, of the originally hostile elements. But this ingenious reconstruction of the history has fallen before the attack of historical investigation itself and the later followers of Tübingen Criticism have been forced to recede from so many essential positions and to minimize the alleged division of the apostolic body in so many particulars that the theory ought to have little weight with students of the New Testament and of post-apostolic literature. For the unity of the apostolic body, and the consequent recognition of Paul, we appeal not only to the New Testament itself, when fairly interpreted, but to the earliest extra-canonical writers,—*e.g.*, to Clement of Rome, writing about the same time with the apostle John (Ad Cor. 5, 44, 47, 49), who appeals expressly to Peter and Paul not only as examples of righteousness, but as reproving that very spirit of rivalry with which modern criticism charges them, and mingles their words together as the commandments of one mind; to Ignatius, writing perhaps only a decade later, who uses this language : " I do not enjoin you as Peter and Paul; they were apostles. I am but a condemned man" (Rom. iv.) ; to Polycarp, whose imitative pen betrays his reverent use of the writings of all the representative apostles; and, passing by many other witnesses, to the extensive statements of Irenæus of Lyons. To be sure these ancient authors were not writing for the express purpose of refuting beforehand modern naturalistic criticism, and occasional difficulties occur in the evidence which have been made the most of. The most recent contention is that the Epistles of Paul were not considered as technically "Scripture" by the Church until the false position in which Marcion and others placed him required his orthodoxy to be vindicated (see Harnack's *Dogmenge-schichte*, i. 304 ; Werner's *Der Paulismus des Irenæus*). But before Marcion wrote, the Epistles of Paul were used in precisely the same manner as other books of the New Testament and must stand or fall with them ; while the idea that Marcion was the first to announce the fact that God had given to the Christian Church a written rule of faith in addition to the Old Testament, attributes far too much originality to that famous heretic. We admit, indeed, that the Church of the second and third centuries did not appropriate the doctrines of grace which Paul taught with anything like his consistency. But that has been no unusual phenomenon in

Christian history. None the less is the evidence ample that, while Paul derived his authority from no man, and while his course was opposed by many Jewish Christians, yet, after the first suspicions were overcome, as the book of Acts relates, the Church recognized his credentials, and that means that the other apostles recognized them, even as he himself declares. If so, then whatever authority on other grounds we attach to the original apostles becomes a corresponding attestation of Paul. Were they merely trustworthy witnesses? They witness to the sufficiency of those of his credentials which we cannot examine. Were they the acknowledged founders of the Church? They acknowledge the apostle of the Gentiles to be a founder too. Were they endowed with the Spirit to be the authoritative teachers as well as founders of the Church? Then they admit also Paul's claim to be the same and his epistles to be part of the Church's abiding rule.

(2). The other argument, drawn from the internal relation which Paul's teaching bears to the rest of Scripture, depends on the results of exegesis.

(*a*). It may be shown that his teaching is a legitimate unfolding of ideas already announced in the teachings of Jesus. In Christ's declaration of the righteousness which must exceed that of the Scribes and Pharisees, of the necessity of his death as a ransom for sin, of the wholly lost condition of mankind, of the necessity of regeneration and of the Father's "drawing," of his peculiarly intimate and vital relation to his people based on the Father's gift of them to him from eternity, of the immediateness and completeness of the reconciliation of God and the sinner through him, and of the necessity of the sinner's dependence upon him for salvation, it is easy to see the elements of Paul's doctrine waiting for some one to arrange them in the light of the full significance of Calvary, and of the person of the risen Lord.

(*b*). It may be shown further that his doctrine stands in such relation of that of the other apostolic writers as to be an integral and necessary part of the apostolic teaching as a whole ; forming the required complement to James, one of the presuppositions of Peter and the author of the Epistle to the Hebrews, and with these laying the foundation on which John stood, with his personal remembrance also of the Lord's discourses, to set forth the true revelation of God and of life with God which the Divine Word had effected and in the disclosure of which the written word was to find its goal. The more closely the doctrines of the several apostolic writers are examined, the more manifest becomes the one, identical truth which, with rich diversities of view, all express ; and in this complex organism of living truth the teaching of Paul appears as the vertebrate column on which the structure of the whole depends.

(*c*). And then it may be shown, finally, that Pauline doctrine, as the apostle himself claimed, is a legitimate unfolding of the teachings of the Old Testament ; a return to Moses and the prophets as against the Scribes and Pharisees ; that he built, not on rabbinical theology, but on the principles imbedded in the Old Testament, and that, strange as his position seemed to the Jews of his day, he did but bring to complete expression the central truths of Israel.

It is not my purpose to do more than indicate these points of internal relationship. Their full working out belongs to Biblical Theology. But the result will, I

believe, be substantially what I have indicated. It is
so in its general features to every careful reader of the
Bible. If so, Paul's Epistles authenticate themselves as
an integral part of that unified and yet diversified collection of literature which we call " the Bible." But that
in turn authenticates him as one of its intended writers.

On these two lines of attestation, the one external,
the other internal, must the New Testament student,
who admits the fact of a supernatural revelation through
Jesus Christ, and who is willing to accept the plain
historical statements of the original witnesses as to
what Jesus did and taught, admit also Paul's claims to
apostleship and his epistles to a place among the authoritative apostolic teaching. Then the particular witness,
which, in these epistles, Paul bore to his apostolic consciousness, must be our guide in determining what the
New Testament, and back of that the whole Bible,
really is.

III. The question then arises, what was Paul's doctrine about the Scripture ? Did he attach the same
conception of authority and inspiration to it that we
have found him to attach to his own teaching, whether
oral or written ?

(1). To answer this, we must first examine his descriptions and use of the Old Testament. His use
of it is abundant. He quotes from it formally. He
introduces its phrases. His language is saturated
with its expressions and figures of speech. He assumes
it to be well known to his readers and an authority
recognized by them. There is no question that he possessed it in the form in which we now have it, in the Hebrew and substantially in the Greek. The names, also,

which he applies to it indicate in general his acceptance
of it, in unison with the Jewish Church, as the divinely
given rule of belief and conduct.   It is "the Scripture,"
called so by pre-eminence, "the Holy Scriptures," "the
prophetic Scriptures," "the law and the prophets"
(Rom. iii. 21), "the sacred writings" (2 Tim. iii. 15).
He called the whole collection also "the law," quoting
under that title from Isaiah (1 Cor. xiv. 21 ; see Rom.
iii. 19) ; and in another place, "the oracles of God"
(τὰ λόγια Rom. iii. 2), a phrase which must not be limited to the direct utterances of God, but must be understood to describe the Scriptures as a whole.   These
titles indicate his general attitude toward the Old Testament.   Strongly as he revolted from the Judaism of
his day, he recognized its Bible as God's gift to the
Church of all time, and applied to it the terms of strict-
est faith and devoutest reverence used by those who acknowledged its authority (Rom. iv. 4).

But not to dwell on these obvious facts, it is important for our purpose to observe the descriptions which
Paul gives of the object of the Old Testament and how
it came to fulfil that object.   He held that the Scripture was expressly written for the purpose of teaching the
Church, both Jewish and Christian, the gospel of Jesus
Christ, and this, of course, involved the assumption that
it had been composed under the special direction of God.
He affirms this, be it noted, of the Scripture as a book.   It
was not written in the interest of a legal way of salvation, though it contained the law ; but it was written in
order that the principles of the gospel might be learned
by those who read it rightly.   Not only did Moses and
the prophets speak from God, but the Sacred Scriptures
themselves were in some way composed under divine

control. He not only affirms with Peter that, "moved by the Holy Ghost *men* spake for God," but that "the Scriptures themselves are inspired by God." Paul plainly recognizes the human authorship of the books, and quotes Moses and David and Isaiah as speaking therein. But not only *through them*, but *in these books* of theirs did God also speak. Many readers notice the first part of Paul's statement, but not the second. God spake "through the prophets *in the Holy Scriptures*" (Rom. i. 2).

Hence we read statements like these. After speaking of the sins and sorrows of Israel in the wilderness, he declares: "Now, these things happened unto them by way of example (typically), and they *were written* for our admonition, upon whom the ends of the ages are come" (1 Cor. x. 11). Here he represents both the facts of Israel's history and the *record* of them as having been expressly designed for our spiritual profit. So again, "For whatsoever things were *written* aforetime were written for our learning, that through patience and through comfort of the Scriptures we might have hope" (Rom. xv. 4). And this pertains, according to Paul, to the use of special phrases; for (Rom. iv. 23) he declared that the particular statement of Genesis that "Abraham *believed* God, and it was reckoned to him for righteousness," was *not written* for his sake alone, but for our sake also. The record, that is, of the great typical justification, was expressly made and in this precise form, for our enlightenment. Even the directions of the Mosaic law were *written* for our sakes (1 Cor. ix. 10); not as if they had had no other immediate reference when originally enacted, but that the recording of them in Scripture was for the purpose of instructing us in the

doctrines or duties of a godly life. Therefore the Scriptures are, so to speak, personified by him,—as when he
writes that "the Scripture, foreseeing that God would
justify the Gentiles by faith, preached the gospel beforehand unto Abraham" (Gal. iii. 8), as well as in the
common formula " Scripture saith." Of course, these
affirmations could only have been made on the supposition that he who secured the production of such a record
and who therefore speaks in its language, was none less
than God. So Paul explicitly affirms, " The Gospel of
God, which he promised afore by his prophets in the
Holy Scriptures" (Rom. i. 1, 2). He thus clearly distinguished between the historical revelations made from
time to time, which like the law, had a temporary purpose, and the composition of the Scriptures. These, indeed, contained the record of those revelations, but, besides that, were *so written* that they might teach for all
time the principles of faith and duty. It was on the
basis of this view that he could write to the Corinthians (1 Cor. iv. 6), that they "must not go beyond the
things that are written "; by which remark he meant to
remind them that the Scriptures were the rule of practice
as well as of faith to every Christian. So, too, he could
write to Timothy of the Scriptures (2 Tim. ii. 15) : " they
are able to make thee wise unto salvation through faith
which is in Christ Jesus." His declarations then cul-
minate in the statement : " Every Scripture," that is, the
whole collection to which he had just referred as the
" sacred writings," and all their parts, " being inspired by
God, is also profitable for teaching, for reproof, for correction, for instruction which is in righteousness, that the
man of God may be complete, furnished completely unto
all good works" (2 Tim. iii. 16, 17). Of this last pas-

sage I will speak presently. I desire now only to point
out that Paul represents not only the Hebrew economy
as designed by God to serve a temporary purpose in the
education of his people, and Moses and the prophets
as having spoken from God, but the Hebrew Scriptures
themselves also as a divinely made book or collection of
books intended to teach the Gospel and an abiding rule
of faith and conduct to the Christian. He affirms not
only that the authors of the Old Testament were media
of revelation, but that the literary product itself, and
as such, was in some way divinely made and given to
the Church.

(2). What light then is thrown upon these formal
statements by Paul's actual use of Scripture?

(*a*). He habitually employs it, in accordance, as I
have already remarked, with his idea of its purpose, to
show that it taught his "Gospel." He does this not by
catching at plausible phrases, or by gleaning here and
there from the Old Testament expressions which imply
his doctrines; but by showing that the Gospel was the
very substance of the Scripture. Christ, as revealed to
the apostles, was the key to the Old Testament. The
unbelieving Jews read the Old Covenant with a veil
upon their hearts (2 Cor. iii. 14, 15), but he—"the veil
having been done away in Christ"—grasped the real
meaning of the prophetic writings. The more closely
we study Paul's use of Scripture the more should we be
filled with admiration at the clearness and penetration
with which he apprehended the essential religious teaching of the passages he cites. Take the great passages,
which I need not quote, in which he uncovers in God's
recorded transactions with Abraham the doctrine of
gracious justification through faith; or the way in which

(Rom. iii.) he presents the Scriptural indictment of man as a sinner by a series of citations from the Psalms and Isaiah so arranged as to set forth in sacred phrase the fact, the practice, the source of human wickedness; or the magnificent argument (Rom. ix.-xi.) wherein he justifies on Scriptural grounds the loss by the Jews of their peculiar privileges.   I do not see how any one can examine Paul's use of Scripture in these classical instances without being convinced that the apostle, so far from juggling with words, penetrated to the very marrow of the law and the prophets.   There are instances, I know, where at first sight he seems to deal with words rather than with thoughts, and to be guilty of fanciful interpretation.   These instances are few in number, but they have been made the most of.   His use (Gal. iv. 21-31) of the story of Sarah and Hagar with their sons; his interpretation (1 Cor. ix. 9, 10; 1 Tim. v. 17, 18) of the Mosaic command, "Thou shalt not muzzle the oxen treading out the corn"; his citation of Isaiah xxviii. 11, "By men of strange tongues will I speak unto this people" (1 Cor. xiv. 21), as bearing on the use by the Church of the miraculous gift of tongues,—are examples, to which as many more might be added. (2 Cor. iii. 14, 15, "When it shall turn unto the Lord, the veil is taken away"; 2 Cor. viii. 15, "As it is written, he that gathereth much," etc., Rom. x. 6-9).   But certainly it is only fair to judge of these instances by the apostle's prevailing habit, and to ask if further examination will not show that below the apparently verbal interpretation there was the perception by him of a principle in each case of which the Old Testament passage was one expression and his application of it another.   I believe that this can be shown in every case, not excepting even the miscalled "allegory" of Hagar and Sarah, and the much misunderstood remark about the unmuzzled ox. It should, moreover, not be forgotten that these interpretations, which are offensive to some, proceed conspicuously on the supposition that the Scripture, as a writing, was a divine work.   But many more examples might be adduced in which Paul's use of Scripture must have been to his first readers like the breaking of sunlight into darkened chambers.   Sometimes by merely a single word he illuminates prophetic language, and again, by a group of passages, he lays bare at one stroke the golden ore which the older revelation contained.

(*b*). But further, he treats the Biblical narrative as true.   This will be denied by none; but it is important to observe how vital the truthfulness of the narrative was to Paul's theological position.   For he conceived of the Gospel as the climax in a series of economies which were particularly ordered by God with a view to the announcement and understanding of it.   He begins commonly with the period of the promise, and then explains the reason of the later introduction of the law. In his analysis of sin, however, he goes back to the first man and distinctly bases his doctrine of justification on the unity of the race in Adam.   It thus appears that the truthfulness of the Old Testament's narrative—so far at least as its leading features are concerned—was fundamental to Paul's view of God's government of the world and of the method of man's salvation.   And so, when alluding to facts stated in the narrative, he always treats them as real.   This is to be particularly noted for the reason that his view of Scripture, which I have described, as written for the spiritual instruction of the later Church, might have led him, as it has led others, to undervalue the historical nature of the facts. It might have, as it did in less accurate hands, transformed Scripture into an allegory. But even when drawing his spiritual lesson from Hagar and Sarah, he manifestly regards the facts related of them as true. So he speaks of the life of Israel in the desert, " These things *happened* unto them (typically or) by way of example." He did not look upon the narrative as an allegory, but as a relation of actual facts, some of which were of vital importance for a right conception of God's dealings with mankind, and so narrated as to set forth, when properly understood, what God intended us to learn. So organic was the relation in his view between the dispensation of the Gospel and the previous history of Israel as set forth in the Scriptures, that only in the light of the latter could it be said, "when the fulness of time was come, God sent forth his Son " (Gal. iv. 4).

(*b*). Still again, he is careful at times to support his argument by an appeal to the precise words used by the Sacred Writers. Did he teach that " Christ has been made a curse for us"? He appeals, in justification of his language, to the language of Deuteronomy, " Cursed is every one that hangeth on a tree " (Gal. iii. 10). He confirms his doctrine of the spiritual Israel by the language of the promise to Abraham, "and to thy seed"; "as of one, even Christ " (Gal. iii. 16). So in the Epistle to the Romans, his appeal frequently lies to the language of Scripture as well as to its real significance. He points out that the Scripture declares that "the just shall live by faith " (i. 17) ; that "Abraham believed God, and it was reckoned to him for righteousness " (iv. 3) ; that circumcision was given him "as a sign " (iv. 11) ; that he was intended to be

the spiritual ancestor of believing Gentiles because
called "the Father of many nations" (iv. 17); that his
spiritual seed should not be identified with his fleshly
descendants because it was written, " In Isaac shall thy
seed be called " (ix. 7); that the Scripture itself applies
the word "hardening" to God's rejection of the repro-
bate (ix. 18). These examples are sufficient to prove
that in Paul's mind the very phraseology of the Scripture was valid for religious argument, and expressed
divine thought.

What then is to be said of certain features of his
quotations which appear to many inconsistent with such
belief in the value of Scripture language? It is a fact
that he often makes his quotations loosely, and occasionally does no more than give their substance. Sometimes, also, he evidently changed the phraseology on
purpose. In a number of instances he differs from the
Septuagint, and sometimes follows the Septuagint
where it differs from the Hebrew, and occasionally differs from both. Many regard these facts as wholly inconsistent with any high valuation of the words of
Scripture. But, aside from the fact that the latter view
would make Paul contradict his own express statements,
the following additional facts deserve consideration.

It is wholly unreasonable to require that even an inspired man, who believed that the words of Scripture
were written under God's direction, should always quote
Scripture with textual exactness. This would be to insist on his becoming a pedant, as if God could not inspire a man to write rhetorically, or poetically, as well as,
when the occasion required, with simple prosaic accuracy. We have only a right to require of Paul, on
his own theory of the inspiration both of Scripture and

himself, that when he declares Scripture to have said a thing, it shall be true that Scripture did say it, and that, when he does argue from the words of Scripture, the words shall be there and his argument from them be in accordance with Scriptural principles. To insist that Paul's doctrine of Scripture, as we have presented it, ought to have precluded him from ever citing the sense rather than the language of the Old Testament, or from ever combining passages together, or from ever failing to correct any bad translation of the Septuagint when the existing translation did not invalidate the force of his appeal, or from changing the language intentionally, when by so doing he could bring out the meaning more strongly for the purpose in hand, is to insist that his epistles, because inspired, should have none of those rhetorical qualities which were the natural manifestation of the apostle's own mental processes.

In reality, however, Paul is remarkably exact, in the great majority of instances, when formally quoting from the Old Testament. The wonder is that his memory served him so well; for of course he could seldom have had the means, if he so desired, of verifying his citations. When he does quote loosely, his argument never depends on the verbal accuracy of his quotation, and he always correctly represents the teaching of Scripture when he professes to do so. His mind, however, was so saturated with Scripture that he seems often to be rather speaking himself in its words than to be citing it, and he continually strives in citing to explain and apply it. Thus in Galatians we find eleven clear quotations. Of these, five (iii. 6, 11, 16; iv. 27; v. 14) are verbally exact, and three (iii. 8, 12, 13) practically so,—(*i. e.*, the differences, chiefly in tense or person or verbal form, are too slight to invalidate the accuracy of the quotation), while the variations in the other three (ii. 16; iii. 10; iv. 30) can be accounted for by the apostle's desire to state the Old Testament teaching in phraseology which would make its real significance clearer to his readers. In 1 Corinthians, out of 27 instances of reference to Old Testament language, only 11 are again formal quotations. Of these, seven are exact or practically so, and three (iii. 19; xiv. 21; xv. 54) indicate either acquaintance with the Hebrew and an intentional correction of the LXX, or else the possession by Paul of a better Greek version than we have. The remaining quotation (ii. 9) is very free, so that some suppose it to have been taken from a lost apocryphal book. But that is a violent hypothesis, opposed to Paul's invariable custom elsewhere; and since the citation expresses Scriptural teaching in Scriptural figures of speech, and since there is a passage in Isaiah (liv. 4) which obviously forms its starting-point, we can only look upon this case as one in which the apostle modified consciously the prophetic declaration in order to apply its principle more forcibly to the matter of which he was writing.

In the Romans there are about 73 quotations and allusions of all kinds. Of these, 27 are exact citations, and 20 practically so. Only 8 could be called loose, 8 are mere allusions, 2 are centos of scattered passages grouped for a purpose. In 4 cases we may observe apparently intentional changes of verbiage to make the bearing of the truth more evident. Seven (i. 17; ix. 1, 7, 32; x. 15; xi. 4, 34; xii. 19) times he differs from the Septuagint, and corresponds more closely to Hebrew. In six (iii. 4, 14; ix. 32; x. 11; xii. 19; xv. 12) instances he follows the Septuagint where it differs from the Hebrew, but in none of these cases does the sense of Script- ure suffer.   Once (xi. 26) he differs in a single word from both Hebrew and Septuagint, saying, " *Out of* Sion shall come the deliverer," instead of " To or for Sion "; but here he apparently mingled a reminiscence of one of the Psalms with the language of Isaiah.

It would be tedious for me to give more details.   I believe these to be fair specimens of the proportion of exact and inexact quotations in Paul's Epistles as well as of his methods.   The key to whatever difficulty remains is found in the fact, which should never be for- gotten, that Paul combined and meant to combine in his use of Scripture the functions of both an appellant and an interpreter.   He is ever bent on letting the light of the Gospel on the Scripture, as well as on supporting the Gospel by the Scripture.   He never pretended that he had derived his doctrine from the Scripture.   He always claimed that he had derived it by revelation from Jesus Christ.   Then, however, he saw the meaning of Scripture, and could both appeal to it and explain it. His exegetical method therefore was determined by his practical purpose.   He had no need, as we have, first to state the "grammatico-historical" sense of the passage quoted, and then to elaborately show the prin- ciple on which it could be applied to the case in hand. When quoting, he often is interpreting.   Hence some of his striking combinations of passages.   Hence his change of its phraseology when occasion required. Hence his attitude now of reverence for its letter, and now of apparent disregard of its letter and attention solely to its essential meaning.   When all these facts are duly considered, there appears nothing in Paul's actual use of Scripture which can be fairly made to contradict his expressed doctrine.

And now in the light of this study we may grasp the meaning which he himself must have meant to convey by the word which in his last epistle he applied to Scripture, —ϑεόπνευστος. It is his own word. It means "breathed into by God." He affirms it not of the writers, but of the sacred writings. These writings are "God in-breathed." The apostle must be his own interpreter, and by the aid of what I have shown is the idea which he embodied in this now classic word to be obtained. By their inspiration he evidently meant that, as writings, they were so composed under God's particular direction that both in substance and in form they were the special utterance of his mind and will. Their words like the apostle's were "pneumatic." The Divine Spirit dwelt in them and breathed through them. And this in no vague, mystic, intangible sense, but in the same sense in which he had said of himself and his fellow-apostles, "We speak not in words which man's wisdom teacheth, but which the Holy Ghost teacheth," and with the same result that the writings were veritably the word of God. *How* the Divine Spirit operated in either case Paul does not say. The fact and its consequences he unmistakably affirms.

I have purposely omitted any appeal to the Epistle to the Hebrews because its authorship is disputed even by evangelical scholars. If, however, it was not written by Paul, it is certainly the utterance of Pauline ideas. When, then, we find in it the Psalmist's words quoted, "To-day if ye will hear his voice," with this formula, "as the Holy Ghost saith,"—and when we observe further that the writer's argument turns in great part on the use in the psalm of the word "to-day,"—we are made doubly sure that our interpretation of Paul's doctrine of Scripture is correct, and that he held it in common with the other Christian teachers of the apostolic age.

Such is the account which to the exegetical student Paul renders of his own inspiration and of that of the Old Testament. That the same is equally true of the other writings of the New Testament will hardly be denied by any who accept Paul's representations. He recognized the authority of the other apostles as of the same nature with his own, and the books which they wrote or gave to the Church must stand on the same level with his or the whole Pauline doctrine of inspiration be given up. He nowhere affirms, be it noted, that inspiration was confined to the apostles, and his recognition of Christian prophets,—as when he declares the Church to be built "on the foundation of apostles and prophets,"—would seem to imply the contrary. But he does make the apostles infallible teachers and the authorized founders of the Church. Those writings therefore which, though not written by apostles, were accepted by the Church from the beginning as part of Scripture, must be regarded as sealed with their authority and therefore also inspired ; and the fact is that in the following century apostolic authority,—direct or indirect,—was the express ground on which the books of the New Testament were received by the Church. That even in the apostolic age itself the conception of a New Testament Scripture had formed, to which the same qualities were attributed which were held to belong to the Old Testament, appears incidentally when Paul cites (1 Tim. v. 18) the saying of our Lord, " The laborer is worthy of his hire " (Luke x. 7) as a saying of Scripture, and when Peter in his second epistle refers to Paul's epistles under the same title. Those who, partly because of these expressions, would deny the genuineness of the Pastoral Epistles and of Second Peter must surely fail to realize what Paul's teaching on the subject of inspired Scripture really was.

IV. Now it is not my place to condense these exegetical results into a dogmatic formula, though I think it obvious what that formula should be. I desire to state in conclusion what, I apprehend, should be the effect of these claims of the Bible on the mind of the Christian scholar as he approaches its study. I say " Christian scholar" because with such alone we are concerned. We are here as confessedly Christian men, and it is not likely that many of us would devote our lives to the study of the Bible, were it not for our settled convictions that its teaching is of supreme value to mankind. But when, in addition to this general conviction, we find it to make such pretensions as I have endeavored to describe, these cannot but impose special requirements upon the student.

Certainly he must approach it with peculiar reverence. It is not like other books. It is not inspired in the sense in which works of genius or spiritual insight are. In its production God was immediately and peculiarly concerned. As our Lord is the Son of God in a sense in which His people are not, though they also in their way are sons of God, so is the Bible His word in a sense which cannot be affirmed even of those other literary products (of which there are many), which contain the truth and manifest the Divine Spirit. Such is the Bible's own account of itself ; and if we may not accept

its account of itself, why should we care to ascertain its
account of other things?

So it is hardly possible for one who realizes this to
go to the study of it in the same mental attitude in
which he would approach other literature. He is dealing with a body which is, he has reason to believe, in
all its parts quick with divine thought and life; and he
cannot use his lens and scalpel on it with ordinary
emotions.

He would, however, utterly misapprehend its character and claims, if his reverence were blind or unintelli-
gent. The inspired Word pretends to be in every sense
a living thing, and, to enter into its secrets, the student
must himself be alive, both intellectually and morally.
He is very far from dealing with a mechanical product.
In its doctrines and its words, in its substance and its
form, in its historical genesis and in its proclamation of
eternal truths, the Bible is an organism,—with its roots
running down into the history, the language, the social,
mental, and religious activity both of the Hebrews and
of the greater world about them,—while yet its mould-
ing, forming principle is derived from above. As I
have said, Paul nowhere describes the *method by* which
the Divine Spirit operated in himself or in the prophets
to produce the Scripture. It is only the fact and the
consequences to which he bears his testimony. The
method we must judge, so far as may be possible, from
the phenomena. These point to a complex process,
wherein many subordinate agents were made to co-oper-
ate with the immediate exercise of divine power. Out
of the matrix of a divinely guided history was this divine
—human book born, and our very faith in its complete
divine vitality should make us eager to apprehend every

human element which entered into its being. Through
the form alone can we reach the substance ; through the
words the thought ; through the historical the doctrinal ;
through the human the divine. Every element of this
complex literary product acquires new interest when we
believe that through them all we are brought into contact with the process in and by which God has revealed
himself and his will to men.

At the same time his reverence for the finished product will keep the student cautious and humble in his
judgments. He will not expect to understand everything
about the construction of the Bible. He will not be
staggered if he find in it statements which he cannot
yet comprehend, or phenomena which he cannot yet explain. He will assuredly trust its statements when they
are clearly ascertained. If his reverence be intelligent
and his examination be critical, as they certainly ought
to be, both his intelligence and his criticism will recog-
nize that the character of the subject examined sets obvious limitations upon their exercise.

(1). But to be more specific, the Bible's account of itself will impress upon the student the great importance of
ascertaining by valid processes the original text. We
know enough of the history of the New Testament
text to perceive that in all that is required for the correct ascertainment of Christian doctrine and duty, God
has "by singular care and providence kept it pure
through all ages." Nevertheless, the student will want
to secure as nearly as possible an absolute reproduction
of the original that he may apprehend the precise thought
of the inspired penman even in its smallest details.
The Bible's account of itself would seem to provide
the strongest incentive to the study of textual criticism.

(2). The same reason also will stimulate to the most exact and painstaking exegesis. To one who accepts the Bible's account of itself, no question, even of grammatical structure, will appear without importance. The usage of words, their origin and their receptiveness of Scriptural thought, the laws governing literary composition of this and of that kind, will be investigated by him with new zeal. Everything will be valued which will enable him to grasp the precise shade of thought in the section before him. It would be an immense mistake for him to become a careless exegete, or to fancy that, because its verbal forms are inspired, he is not to strive to grasp the very thought which is in them,—or to suppose that, because in all its parts it is inspired, he is not to carefully observe from it the proportion of truth and to grasp its teaching as a whole,—or to allow his spiritual fancy to interpret Scripture as the exigencies of the pulpit may seem to require. This was the fault of much of exegesis in the ancient Church ; and though it was based on a correct doctrine of Scripture, and was meant to do honor to the inspired Word, it wrought for ages injury to the truth and hid, while it pretended to unfold, the word of God. We should rather conclude from the inspiration of Scripture, that every statement of it is to be apprehended with precise accuracy,—is to be seen to be just what it exactly is, if the divine thought in it and the relation of its thought to others, and so the complex thought of the whole is to be really learned. They who accept and teach a wholly inspired Bible ought to count no labor too great to ascertain, by the use of every critical instrument as well as by devout sympathy with both the human and the divine authors, the exact meaning of the book.

(3). And then, building on precise exegesis, interpreting according to the natural rules of the various kinds of literary composition, the student will move through the Bible from its beginning to its close,—feeling his way, as it were, from fibre to fibre, from part to part, of this living organism,—until he approaches to an apprehension of it as a whole, perceives its structural unfolding and its vital principle, and is thus enabled to enter into the fulness of its content. Such a student should not be surprised, if he discover that elements, historical or verbal or doctrinal, which enter into the structure of the Bible, had a previous existence of their own. There is an economy observable in all God's operations whereby he uses existing materials for new purposes rather than creates similar ones, and the entirely unmechanical view of inspiration which we have gleaned from the Bible makes it even probable that in some cases (for example in the Synoptic Gospels) a valid literary criticism may discern pre-existing materials. But the student who accepts the Bible's account of itself must admit that only as incorporated in the Scripture can such materials be affirmed to be inspired ; and while such investigations may interest and instruct him, he will feel it to be his chief duty to apprehend aright the teaching of the Bible itself. He will feel that only by entering into its thought, as that is progressively unfolded in the Bible, will he be able to use the book for the supreme purposes for which it claims to have been given.

Some one will say, perhaps, that in entering on my professorial work, I ought to have emphasized the human side of Scripture rather than the divine side, —since the examination of the Bible on its human side has in modern times proved so rich a blessing to the Bible-using Church. I have no intention of forgetting this. But there is now no danger, as once there was, of our undervaluing the human side. The danger lies in our failing to perceive the definite claims which the Bible makes for itself; in our failing to perceive that, even though human, it is also divine, and this, not in a vague, indefinable way, but in the distinct sense that, as a literary product, and in all the parts thereof, it is animated by the thought and moulded by the intention of the Divine Spirit. The danger lies in our thinking that the admission of this is to introduce a mechanical conception of God's handiwork, and is inconsistent with the rich variety of thought and language by which the Bible is obviously marked; whereas it is rather the strongest stimulus to devout, critical investigation, while the limits which it puts upon criticism are only those which loyalty to the abundant evidence that the Scriptures do speak from God would naturally dictate. As divine, has the Bible been bequeathed to us by the apostles. As such, it is more worthy of lifelong study than on any other supposition it could possibly be. As such, its humanity, if I may so speak, becomes the priceless treasure that it is. As such, it occupies the place it does alike in theological discipline, in the Church, and in human history. As such, and only as such, does it provide that which nothing else provides,—a rock, on which man's feet may stand amid the shifting sands of thought and while the mist of ignorance,—dimly lit by guesses, hopes, and fears,— still hides the sun.

www.ingramcontent.com/pod-product-compliance
Lightning Source LLC
Chambersburg PA
CBHW031816090426
42739CB00008B/1297